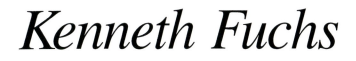

Kenneth Fuchs

American Rhapsody

Romance for Violin and Orchestra

PIANO REDUCTION

ISBN 978-1-4803-3154-9

EDWARD B.
MARKS MUSIC
COMPANY

Exclusively Distributed By

HAL•LEONARD®
CORPORATION
7777 W. BLUEMOUND RD. P.O. BOX 13819 MILWAUKEE, WI 53213

www.ebmarks.com
www.halleonard.com

To John Thomas Dodson, in warm friendship

Solo Violin
Flute
English Horn
Clarinet in B♭
Bassoon
Horn in F
Trumpet in C
Trombone
Percussion (2 players)
Glockenspiel, Suspended Cymbal
Harp
Strings

———————————

Duration: 9 minutes, 30 seconds

———————————

American Rhapsody is a lyrical concerto for violin and orchestra. The work takes its creative impulse from the first few measures of the second movement of my composition *Where Have You Been? (String Quartet No. 2)*. The principal melody and accompanying harmonies of that work, composed in 1993, provided the starting point for musical development in this concerto.

The impressionistic musical language of *American Rhapsody* is created from a melodically arpeggiated minor eleventh chord presented by the solo violin in its opening phrase. The wide-ranging melodic arc of the solo violin theme, as well as the widely-spaced pan-diatonic harmonies of the work, have an open quality suggesting the stylistic elements of mid-Twentieth Century American composers from whom I continue to draw inspiration. The work is cast in a continuously evolving single movement. The soloist serves as the catalyst for symphonic development of the musical ideas through interaction with various players and sections of the orchestra.

American Rhapsody was composed at the request of my friend and colleague, conductor John Thomas Dodson. We first met as undergraduate students in 1976, and the journey of a long friendship through music has been one of joyful discovery. The work was composed during a two-week period in July 2008 in Mansfield Center, Connecticut.

— Kenneth Fuchs

Performance rights administered by ASCAP

Rental materials are available from:
Theodore Presser Company
588 North Gulph Road
King of Prussia, Pennsylvania 19406
Tel: (610) 592-1222 • Fax: (610) 592-1229
www.presser.com

Duration: 9:30

for John Thomas Dodson, in warm friendship

American Rhapsody

Romance for Violin and Orchestra

KENNETH FUCHS

Andante tranquillo ♩ = 60

Solo Violin

Piano

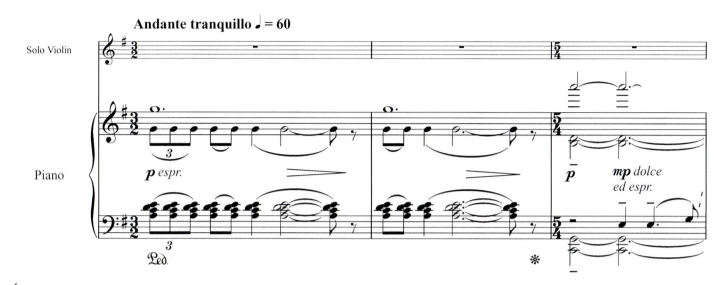

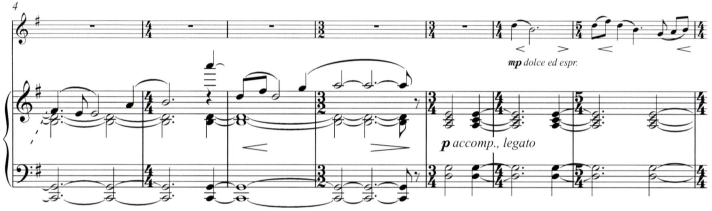

Più mosso ♩ = 66
(poco precipitando)

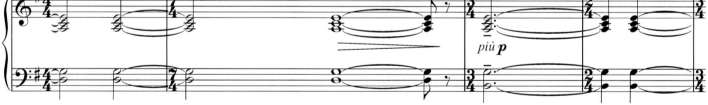

poco accel. . . . .

cresc. poco a poco

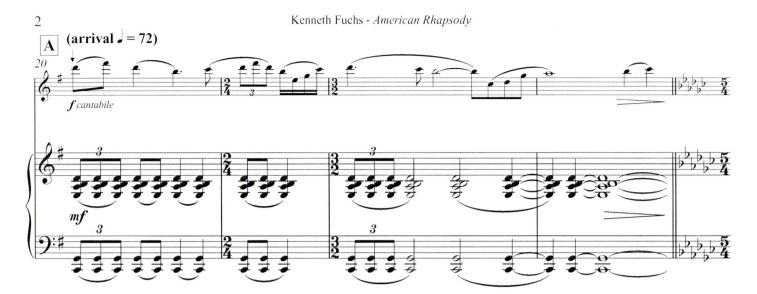

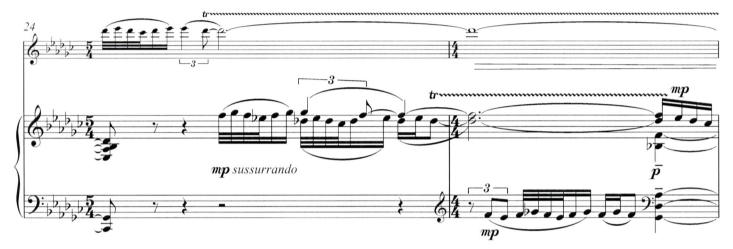

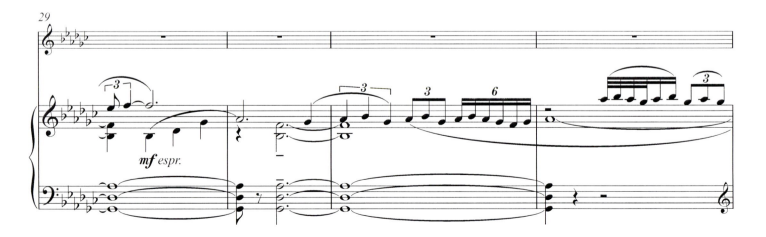

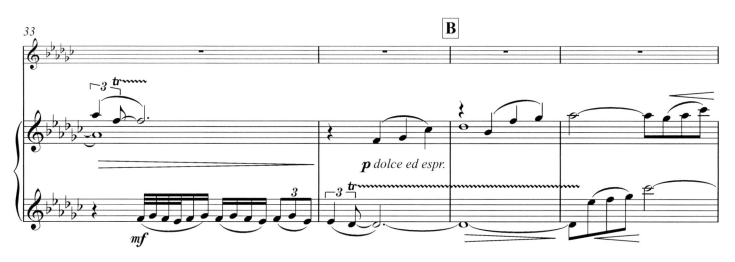

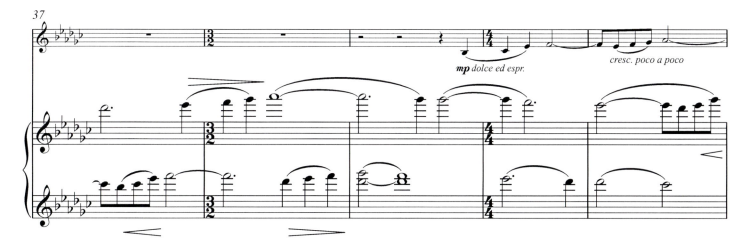

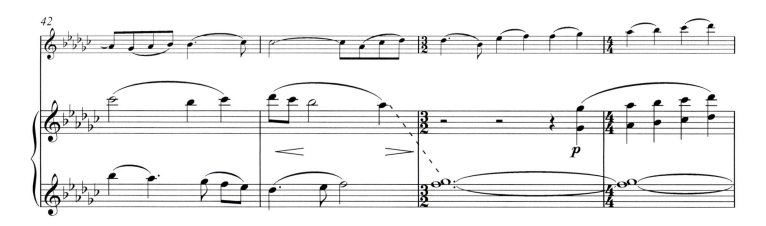

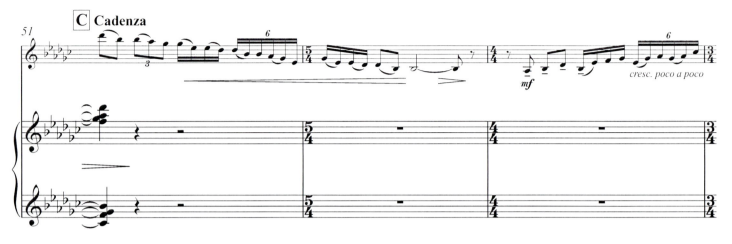

Solo Violin

for John Dodson, in warm friendship

AMERICAN RHAPSODY
Romance for Violin and Orchestra

KENNETH FUCHS

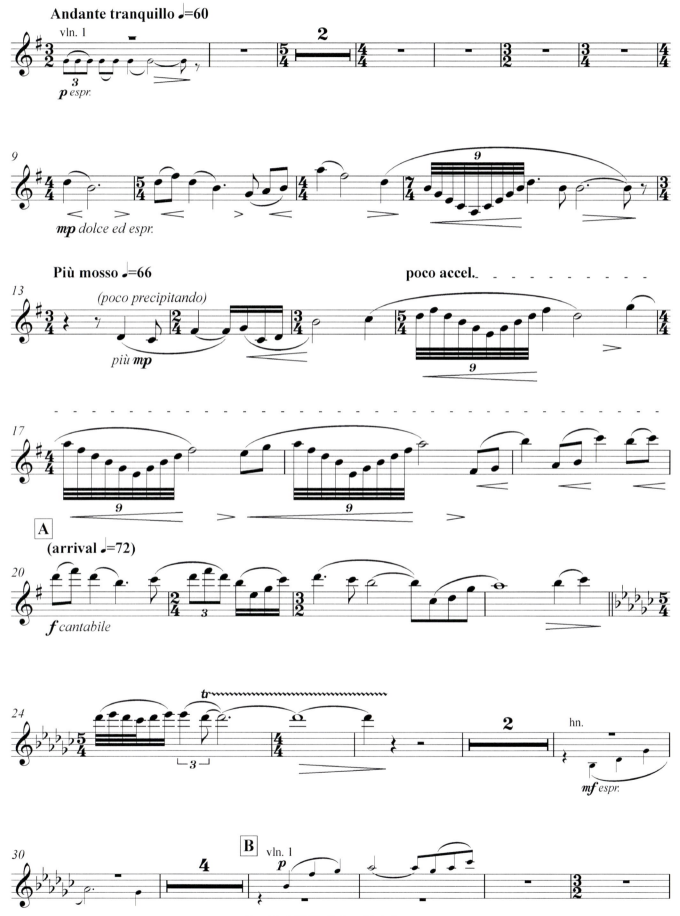

C Cadenza

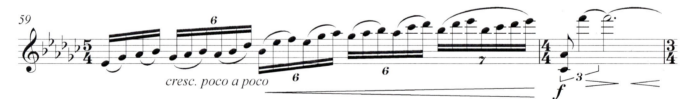

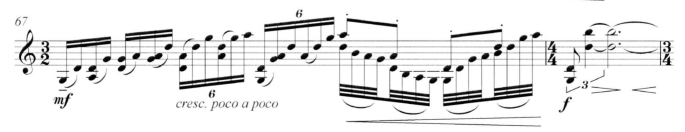

SHELVING
8/12/2024

Qty: 1

Location:
70-02-017-03-_

Customer PO #:
ETZ09488190

Title:
American Rhapsody

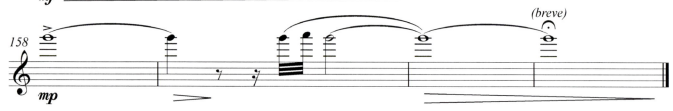

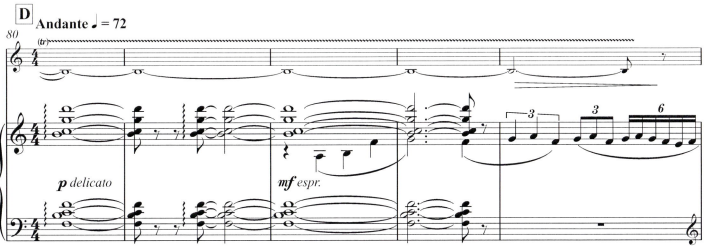

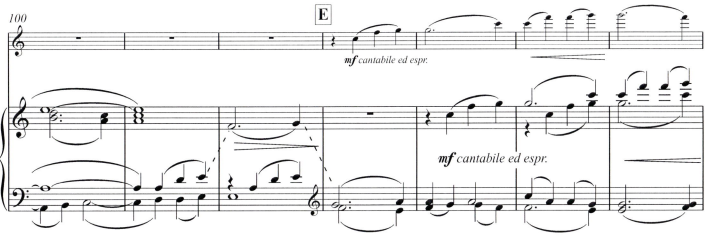

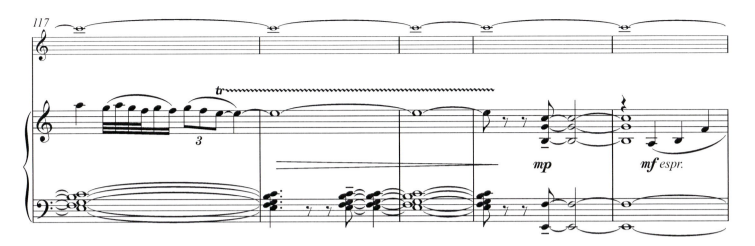

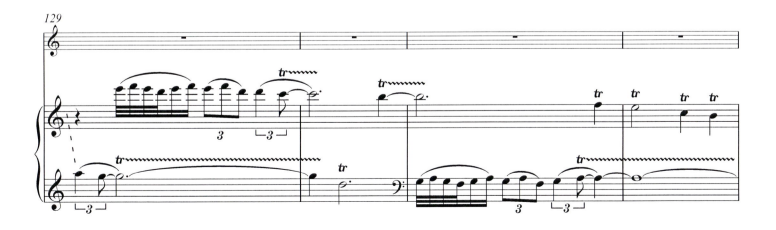

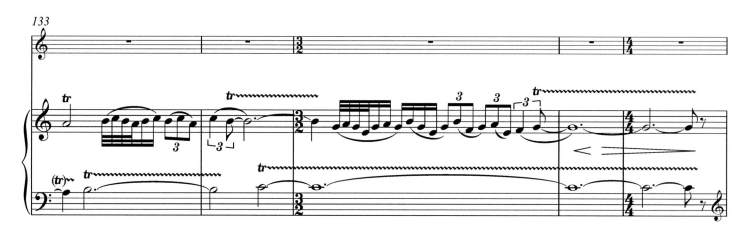

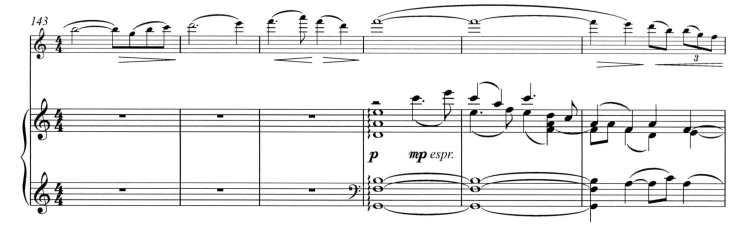

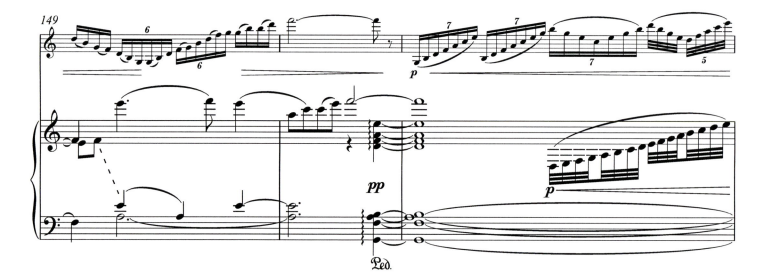

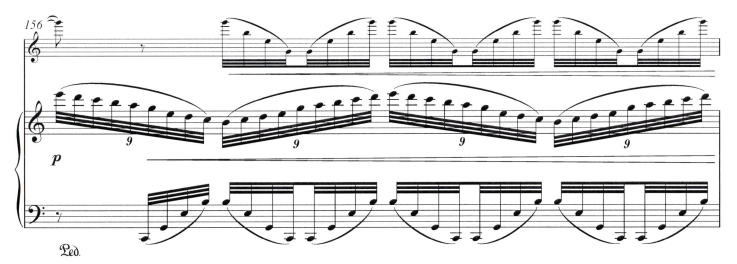

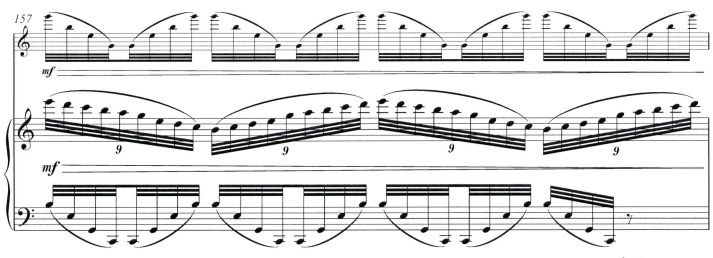

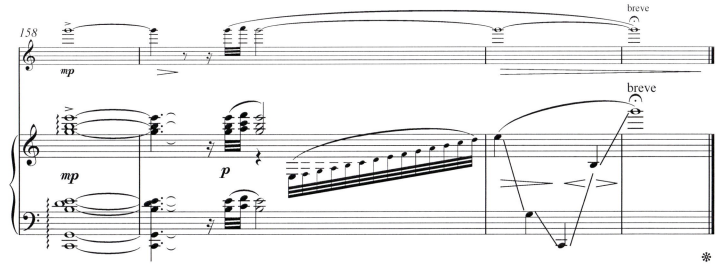